CONTENTS

INTRODUCTION

PLEASING A KING

In 1603 William Shakespeare and his colleagues at the Globe Theatre were at the height of their popularity. Known as the Chamberlain's Men, they were under the protection of the Lord Chamberlain, the organiser of entertainment at court, and were often asked to play for the Queen herself. The Lord Chamberlain was a man of power in the strictly controlled world of plays and playhouses. His office granted companies licenses to perform. He demanded changes to plays if he thought they would offend the Queen. Actors and writers had even been imprisoned if they went too far. Generally, though, the Chamberlain's Men knew how to keep on the right side of those in power. Their professional survival depended on it.

A NEW REIGN

Queen Elizabeth I died childless at Richmond-on-Thames on 24 March 1603. News travelled fast and by 5 April her successor, King James VI of Scotland, was leaving Edinburgh to be crowned King James I of England. James had become King of Scotland at the age of three, when Elizabeth had deposed his mother, Mary Queen of Scots. He was widely read and wrote poetry and books on a range of subjects. He was determined to show himself a wise and firm king. Shortly after arriving in London, James took the Chamberlain's Men under his wing and they were renamed the King's Men. They probably took part in his coronation procession in 1604. They played before the King about ten times a year, and above all they relied on his support and protection.

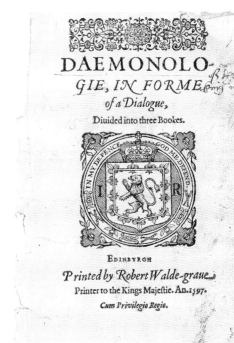

The frontispiece to King James I's book, *Daemonologie*, 1597.

Robert Winter · Christopher Wright · John Wright · Thomas Percy · Guido Fawkes · Robert Catesby · Thomas Winter

Bates

During the 35 years of his reign in Scotland, James had learned to survive plots, rebellions and riots. He was so terrified he would be assassinated that he wore specially padded clothes to protect himself. Indeed, within two years several plots to kill him were uncovered. The most famous was the Gunpowder Plot of 1605. James knew who to blame – the conspirators were all Roman Catholics. At this time the official religion of England was Protestant, and many feared a takeover by Catholic Spain. James was convinced that he had been chosen by God to be king and that anyone plotting against him must be in league with the devil. Witchcraft was seen as a real threat to society. In fact James had written a book about it in 1597, called *Daemonologie,* and thought he was an expert on the subject. The King saw witches and Catholic plotters as two of his greatest enemies.

MACBETH

Macbeth was probably written in early 1606, when plots against the King seemed to be everywhere. Shakespeare presents a man who is told by three witches that he will be king and is then encouraged by his wife to bring it about by killing the King. He shows what King James most feared. And when in the play the murderers suffer torments of conscience and are eventually destroyed by the forces of good, the King of England would have been pleased. But we underestimate both Shakespeare and King James if we think that *Macbeth* was only written to please the King. It is a play which asks many difficult questions about ambition, guilt, conscience, and the nature of evil.

THE SOURCES

Early in his career, while Elizabeth was on the throne, Shakespeare had written a series of plays about English history. They had shown England descending into civil war – the Wars of the Roses – from which it was rescued by Henry Tudor, Queen Elizabeth's grandfather, who became King Henry VII. Shakespeare showed that Elizabeth's family, the Tudors, had the best claim to the throne, both legally and morally.

Shakespeare's history plays make great use of Raphael Holinshed's *Chronicles of England, Scotland and Ireland*, an account so popular that it was printed in 1577 and again in an expanded version in 1587. In 1606, with the new king to please, Shakespeare opened his copy of Holinshed once more, turning to the story of the murder of **King Duncan of Scotland** and the evil reign of **Macbeth**.

A portrait of King James I of England by John de Critz, 1610.

BUILDING THE PLOT

Shakespeare does not simply repeat Holinshed's story, in which Macbeth and **Banquo** conspire to assassinate King Duncan. How could he? King James claimed to be descended from Banquo; to connect him with King Duncan's killer would be no way to make friends and influence people. So Shakespeare drew on another Scottish story in Holinshed: the murder of King Duff while a guest in his assassin's house.

From this, and from another version of the Macbeth story in George Buchanan's *History of Scotland*, Shakespeare began to find the character of **Lady Macbeth**, pushing her husband on to the murder.

Yet another history of Scotland, by Bishop John Leslie (1578), describes 'devils' disguised as women telling Macbeth that Banquo's royal descendants will include the family of King James himself. Of course Shakespeare's much wider reading – about witchcraft, guilty conscience, and of the Latin plays of Seneca – and his knowledge of current events, especially the Gunpowder Plot, added to the story. However, part of his plan was to present King James as rightful king of England, and a good and wise ruler.

In August 1606, *Macbeth* was probably played before King James and King Christian I of Denmark by Shakespeare's company. We cannot be sure that this was its first performance, though it is likely. It was certainly performed on the outdoor stage of the Globe Theatre in Southwark where it was seen in April 1611 by Simon Forman, a London doctor and astrologer, who described it in his *Book of Plays*.

In writing *Macbeth* Shakespeare was, as usual, adapting material from several sources. He was not simply using history as found in the *Chronicles,* but giving it a slant that would flatter and interest the King. He had learnt how to please an audience and how to survive in dangerous times.

An engraving of Macbeth, Banquo and the witches, from Raphael Holinshed's *History of Scotland*, 1577.

THE CHARACTERS

Macbeth played by Bob Peck at the Royal Shakespeare Company, 1982.

Three Weird Sisters are the witches who tell Macbeth he will be king, and that Banquo will be the father of kings. 'Weird' does not mean 'strange' as we would use it, but that they are women who know someone's fate or destiny (from *wyrd*, an Old English word).

King Duncan of Scotland is murdered by Macbeth.

Malcolm is his eldest son, later Prince of Cumberland, who escapes to England after his father's murder.

Donalbain is Duncan's younger son, who escapes to Ireland after his father's death.

A Captain in Duncan's army, who describes Macbeth's bravery in the battle.

Macbeth is thane (lord) of Glamis, who will be made thane of Cawdor. He becomes King of Scotland after murdering Duncan.

Lady Macbeth is his wife.

Banquo is a Scottish thane, at first Macbeth's friend and fellow general, later murdered on Macbeth's orders.

Fleance is his son, who escapes when his father is killed.

Macduff is thane of Fife. He kills Macbeth in the last battle.

Lady Macduff is murdered on Macbeth's orders.

Macduff's son is murdered with his mother.

Lennox, Ross, Angus, Caithness, Menteith are Scottish thanes.

A Porter is the gatekeeper at Macbeth's castle.

Seyton is Macbeth's servant.

There are **Three Murderers**.

A Doctor who attends Lady Macbeth.

A Woman who is servant to Lady Macbeth.

Siward is an English lord, Earl of Northumberland.

Young Siward is his son, killed by Macbeth in the last battle.

An English Doctor

Hecate is queen of the witches.

There are **three More Witches**, who are companions of Hecate.

Three Apparitions:
  A Head
  A Bloody Child
  A Child wearing a crown

A Spirit like a Cat
Other Spirits
A procession of **Eight Kings**

The play also calls for an **old man, a messenger**, **murderers**, **servants** and **soldiers**.

David Troughton as The Porter in the Royal Shakespeare Company's 1987 production.

WHAT HAPPENS
IN THE PLAY

THE WEIRD SISTERS MEET

The play opens with a short but spectacular scene of the three witches meeting in thunder and lightning to arrange their next gathering. They decide to get together later that day, after the battle, on a heath (wide, open land) where they know they will find **Macbeth**.

THE REBELLION IS CRUSHED

Two Scottish thanes (lords), Macdonald and Cawdor, have rebelled against their king with help from the King of Norway. **King Duncan** has sent an army led by his loyal thanes to defeat them. News reaches Duncan that the battle is won.

The hero of the day is Macbeth, who killed the traitor Macdonald. Duncan gives orders that Cawdor is to be executed and that Macbeth will be rewarded with his title and position.

MACBETH AND THE WEIRD SISTERS

The three witches meet and exchange stories of torments. When Macbeth and **Banquo** stumble across them, the witches greet Macbeth as Thane of Glamis, which he is, as Thane of Cawdor, which he doesn't yet understand, and, most extravagant of all, as the future king. Banquo is hailed as the founder of a line of kings. The witches vanish. **Ross** and **Angus**, messengers from King Duncan, arrive, praising Macbeth and conferring on him the title, Thane of Cawdor. Banquo is cautious in believing that the truth of the witches' prophecy means that they are good. Macbeth is more deeply affected. Has he already been dreaming he could be king?

Macbeth (Ian McKellen), Banquo (John Woodvine) and the witches (Marie Kean, Judith Harte and Susan Dury) in the Royal Shakespeare Company's 1976 production, directed by Trevor Nunn.

The majestic King Duncan (Griffith Jones) surrounded by his court in Trevor Nunn's 1976 production at the RSC.

MALCOLM IS NAMED HEIR

Duncan presides over a gathering of all his thanes and his two sons, **Malcolm** and **Donalbain**. Macbeth and Banquo are honoured for their bravery, and then Duncan announces that he has chosen his eldest son, Malcolm, as his heir. Macbeth realises that this is a block to his ambition for more power. The royal party sets out for Macbeth's castle at Inverness. This is a sign of favour – it was an honour to receive the King as a guest.

LADY MACBETH'S AMBITION

At Inverness, **Lady Macbeth** has had a letter from her husband about the witches' prophecy. Her mind moves fast. She doubts that Macbeth has the strength of purpose for the violent actions necessary to achieve his ambitions. She calls on spirits to replace all womanly gentleness and pity with 'direst cruelty'. On Macbeth's arrival she speaks the unspeakable: Duncan will never leave their castle alive. She urges her husband to be cunning and deceitful. She wants the crown for him come what may; he is less certain. Duncan arrives and Lady Macbeth greets him graciously.

THE MURDER

Macbeth is plagued by his conscience. He knows that their plan is wrong and is afraid of being found out. His wife taunts him, saying that if he is a real man he'll go through with it. That night Macbeth murders Duncan, then Lady Macbeth plants the knives on his sleeping attendants. When the murder is discovered Macbeth kills them so there are no possible witnesses. Malcolm and Donalbain flee for safety to England and Ireland.

THE EFFECTS OF A GUILTY CONSCIENCE

Macbeth is the most powerful thane and will become king now Malcolm has fled. But he has no peace or security. So that the witches' prophecy about Banquo being the founder of a line of kings will not come true, he sets killers to murder him and his son, Fleance. They botch the job, though, killing Banquo but allowing Fleance to escape.

At a grand feast for all the court Macbeth sees Banquo's ghost and is terrified. Lady Macbeth tries to cover over Macbeth's tell-tale behaviour but finally has to send everyone home before the truth becomes obvious. Relations between husband and wife are strained as Macbeth retreats into a state of terror.

THE WITCHES' PREDICTION

He turns to the witches again for help. They conjure up a parade of future kings: the descendants of Banquo. The only comfort for Macbeth is the witches' promise that he will be king until Birnam Wood moves towards his castle of Dunsinane and that 'none of woman born' can kill him.

As woods don't move and all men are born of women, he thinks he is safe. But Macbeth goes on killing to remove all opposition and his murderers swoop on the defenceless family of **Macduff**, who is in England with Malcolm.

A portrait by John Singer Sargent of Ellen Terry as Lady Macbeth at the Lyceum Theatre, London, 1888.

MALCOLM FORMS AN ARMY

At the English court, Macduff asks Malcolm to raise an army and win back the throne. Malcolm is cautious but when he sees Macduff's despair at the thought that there is no good man to lead Scotland, he comes clean. In fact Malcolm has already negotiated an army with the English King. As they agree to set out together to attack Macbeth, the Thane of Ross arrives and tells Macduff that his family is dead. Macduff's grief turns to anger.

LADY MACBETH DESPAIRS

Lady Macbeth's nerve cracks. She has nightmares and talks about the murder as she sleepwalks, washing imaginary blood from her hands.

The Scottish thanes opposed to Macbeth meet up with the army led by Malcolm and Macduff. Macbeth is defiant but almost at once things begin to go wrong. He is told that his wife has killed herself, then a messenger arrives to tell him that Birnam Wood appears to be moving towards the castle. (The advancing English army has torn down branches to camouflage themselves.) Macbeth senses disaster but rushes out to face his enemies.

MACBETH IS KILLED

Macbeth meets young **Siward**, son of the Earl of Northumberland. They fight and the young man is killed. But then he comes up against Macduff. He taunts Macduff with the witches' prophecy that 'none of woman born' can kill him. Macduff replies that he was not 'of woman born' but delivered by Caesarian section. They fight and Macbeth is killed.

After the battle Macduff returns to Malcolm with Macbeth's head so all can see that the tyrant is dead. The thanes proclaim Malcolm king and he promises a new peace for Scotland.

Macbeth and the witches summon up the spirits. Royal Shakespeare Company, 1976.

THE THEMES

Shakespeare wrote four plays which are known as tragedies: *Hamlet*, *Othello*, *King Lear* and *Macbeth*. Each of these shows the decline of the central character – the hero – from a position of security to catastrophe. The suffering unleashed not only leads to the hero's death but also affects everyone else. Shakespeare's tragedies look at the dark depths of human experience: betrayal, cruelty, jealousy, ambition, power, murder and revenge. These plays are not comfortable; there is little sense of justice and no easy source of hope. Many characters suffer far more than they seem to deserve. Major questions are raised: about how far we are responsible for our own actions or simply the puppets of blind fate; about good and evil; and about the consequences of behaving well or badly.

CHOICE

Macbeth is a play about choice. It spotlights human beings on a knife edge: decisions are made, the consequences unfold and we see that in human action there is a chain of cause and effect. But there is also a larger, more mysterious and frightening aspect to the world of this play. The supernatural keeps breaking through, often in terrifying and violent forms, and there are times when **Macbeth** seems a victim as well as a tyrant.

FATE

Macbeth and **Banquo** are told by the witches that certain things will happen, but not how they will come about, and they are given no hint of the consequences. Must Macbeth take action in order to be king? Will he be a good or a bad king?

The company (including the young Laurence Olivier, fourth from the right) in H.K.Ayliff's production, set in the First World War, London 1928.

Could he turn his back on the **Weird Sisters** and reject what they are offering? In other words, can Macbeth choose, or have the 'decisions' already been taken? And later, when **Lady Macbeth** taunts him with cowardice for his reluctance to kill **Duncan**, is she acting with eyes wide open, fully aware of the consequences, or is she, too, at the mercy of a blind, malevolent fate?

Of course it might be that the Weird Sisters recognised Macbeth's ambition. They knew that some people cannot resist the temptations of gaining and keeping power. As Banquo says to them:

> *'My noble partner*
> *You greet with present grace*
> *and great prediction*
> *Of noble having and of royal hope,*
> *That he seems rapt withal. To me*
> *you speak not.'*

But we still have to ask how far the Macbeths are responsible for what they do. In the end Shakespeare seems to be saying that we must all take responsibility for our actions. There are temptations, opportunities, parts of our characters, relationships with others, which seem to drive us down certain paths. Yet we can always choose. But how many people, when shown what Macbeth is shown by the Weird Sisters, would turn away?

Macbeth's conscience never lets him forget the difference between what he should have done and what he did do. He should have been a loyal subject of King Duncan and accepted Malcolm as heir. He should not have killed the King. But he has given way to Lady Macbeth's goading, and her belief that they'll get away with it. He suffers the torments of conscience and is troubled by questions of right and wrong.

Macbeth (Derek Jacobi) and Lady Macbeth (Cheryl Campbell) after the killing of Duncan in a 1994 Royal Shakespeare Company production.

APPEARANCE AND REALITY

Macbeth and Lady Macbeth embark on a career of murder because they have convinced themselves that Macbeth should be king. But as Macbeth carries out more murders to secure his position, a great gap opens up between the way he and his wife must appear in public and their private world of fear and guilt.

When Lady Macbeth urges her husband to kill Duncan, she thinks they can leave their consciences behind. But she is mistaken. Right from the beginning Macbeth knows that what he is doing is wrong. For a time his ambition lets him ignore his wrong-doing, but in the end he is wracked with guilt.

A WORLD OF OPPOSITES

The imagery of the play is often about pairs of opposites: night and day; darkness and light; the saintly King Edward of England and 'devilish' Macbeth; sleep and sleeplessness: 'Macbeth hath murdered sleep'. But it is also about confusions: 'fair is foul and foul is fair'; 'so fair and foul a day I have not seen'. By their actions, Macbeth and his wife plunge themselves and Scotland into a nightmare world where what should be clear is confused.

Yukio Ninagawa's production at the National Theatre in London in 1987.

This confusion is powerfully expressed in the banquet scene following Macbeth's coronation, where Banquo's ghost appears to the new king. There is tremendous dramatic tension between Lady Macbeth's desperate efforts to maintain the façade of a formal celebration and Macbeth's terror at being confronted by the reality of his murderous actions.

Macbeth is trapped by his guilty conscience and at times Lady Macbeth cannot escape feelings of pity. For her husband's sake, she has tried to push down any normal human emotion – early in the play she asks for all motherly feelings to be taken from her. But she still pities King Duncan, saying she would have killed him herself if he hadn't reminded her of her father. In the end she cannot live with herself. She has nightmares and sleepwalks, trying to wash blood from her hands:

> **'...all the perfumes of Arabia will not sweeten this little hand.'**

Neither Macbeth nor his wife can get the blood off their hands. In desperation, Lady Macbeth kills herself. As he hears of his wife's death, Macbeth realises the futility of what he has done.

> **'Life's but a walking shadow, a poor player**
> **That struts and frets his hour upon the stage,**
> **And then is heard no more.'**

He faces his last battle with great courage.

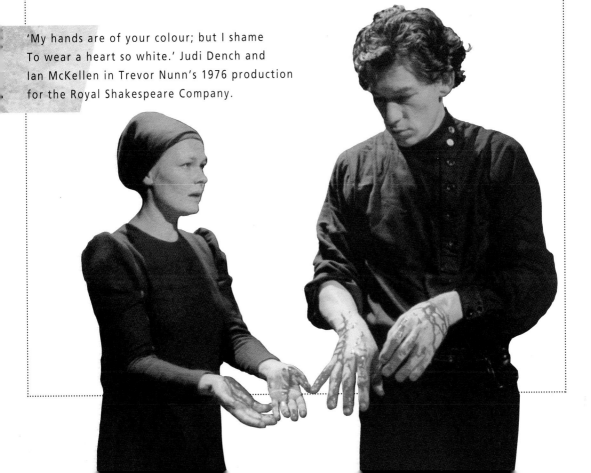

'My hands are of your colour; but I shame To wear a heart so white.' Judi Dench and Ian McKellen in Trevor Nunn's 1976 production for the Royal Shakespeare Company.

PAST PRODUCTIONS

Oliver Cromwell and his Puritan government closed public theatres in 1642. With the restoration of the monarchy in 1660, two theatres were opened in London and many of Shakespeare's plays returned to the stage, usually rewritten to meet changes in taste.

William Davenant's production of *Macbeth* included music and dancing as well as 'flying' witches. This version remained popular until it was replaced by that of David Garrick, the most famous actor of his day, who first played **Macbeth** on 7 January 1744. Although his production was nearer to Shakespeare's original than Davenant's, Garrick still made many changes. **The Porter** (omitted by Davenant on the grounds of bad taste) was replaced by 'a respectable servant', the murders of **Lady Macduff** and her son were not shown, and there was a long dying speech for Macbeth. This *Macbeth* was performed 96 times between 1744 and 1776, although Garrick's last performance was on 22 September 1768.

Macbeth continued to be popular with audiences, and playing the central characters was seen as a great opportunity for actors to make an impact. At the beginning of the nineteenth century Sarah Siddons was a legendary **Lady Macbeth**. Throughout the nineteenth century, the great actor-managers John Philip Kemble, Edmund Kean, William Macready and Herbert Beerbohm Tree put on productions that played on the fascination of the English for romantic Scotland: instead of English military uniforms, the characters wore tartan and carried claymores.

A seventeenth-century production with Thomas Betterton (far right) as Macbeth, with the witches, apparitions and the ghost of Banquo.

A painting by John Jackson
showing William Macready
as Macbeth.

There has been a rich variety of productions of *Macbeth* in the twentieth century. In 1921, in New York, Arthur Hopkins directed a version in a setting which was deliberately not realistic but strong on atmosphere. Powerful beams of light cut across triangles and arches to suggest a frenzied world in which the action unfolded. Less successful was a 1926 London production which transferred the battlefields of the First World War to Scotland. At Stratford, in 1936, Theodore Komisarjevsky's bold production included a set made from aluminium; the witches were hags robbing bodies on the battlefield and **Banquo**'s ghost was Macbeth's shadow. In the same year, in New York, Orson Welles set the play in Haiti, using a cast of 130 black actors and including witch-doctors and voodoo.

Orson Welles returned to the play again in 1948, this time on film. Other films have included *Joe Macbeth* (1955), set in a Chicago gang-war and the Samurai *Throne of Blood*, directed by Akira Kurosawa in 1957, which explores the barbaric mind of Macbeth through striking visual images. Shakespeare's story has also been the basis for three operas: by Guiseppe Verdi in 1847, Ernst Bloch in 1910 and by Dmitri Shostakovitch in 1934 – *Lady Macbeth of the Mtsensk District*. This is built on an interpretation of the character of Lady Macbeth. The heroine takes a lover, murders her husband, then kills herself while being taken to the penal colonies of Siberia. Its bleak plot adapts the themes of Shakespeare's tragedy to the lives of Russian peasants: tragedy is not just for kings and lords.

Strangest of all was Barbara Gerson's 1966 adaptation *Macbird!* which imagined parallels between the assassinations of King Duncan and President John F. Kennedy. *Macbeth* is one of Shakespeare's most frequently performed plays around the world. Its themes never fail to interest actors, directors and audiences.

DIRECTORS' PERSPECTIVES

In recent years, British productions have usually stressed the intense, disturbed world inside the minds of **Macbeth** and his wife. Some productions around the world, however, have made political points, either by using modern dress and settings to focus on issues of power in different political regimes, or by identifying Macbeth and **Lady Macbeth** with recognisable political leaders. This can take some courage, as in the case of a production in Manila in the Philippines, where the actors' costumes copied the dress of President and Mrs Imelda Marcos, the recently deposed leader and his extravagant wife.

At the RSC, two directors in particular have made their mark with strong productions of the play – Trevor Nunn and Adrian Noble. Both have directed it more than once: Trevor Nunn's 1974 production reeked with images of black magic. Christian symbols such as the cross were reversed or turned upside down and we were clearly in a world where the **Weird Sisters'** influence had poisoned everything, turning 'fair' into 'foul'. Trevor Nunn's next version, in 1976, took place in the small studio theatre in Stratford. The actors performed inside a black circle with the audience sitting around them only a few feet away. This closeness of the audience to the action, and the bare setting, focused on the psychological study of personalities cracking apart. One critic said, 'I have never seen the play come across with such throat-grabbing power.'

The Weird Sisters scavenging on the battlefield. Royal Shakespeare Company,1986.

Lady Macduff (played by Penny Downie) and her children in Adrian Noble's 1986 production.

Adrian Noble's first production of *Macbeth* for the RSC in 1986 played down the supernatural, making it less extraordinary. This was not a stage full of symbols of religion or black magic but closer to our own lives. The witches were human rather than supernatural creatures, picking over the battlefield for treasures. One carried a smudge of red in her hand with which she marked Macbeth's forehead. So from a fairly ordinary beginning came the full descent of a human being into disaster.

Directors have always made cuts in the text of a play, whether, like Davenant in the seventeenth century, to get rid of things that seemed in bad taste, or to focus the themes more tightly and cut out what may seem unimportant.

Some scholars believe that the 1623 text of *Macbeth* is itself the result of cuts made in early performances.

In his 1994 RSC production, Adrian Noble not only made cuts, but also reordered some events. Changes were made to enable the story of Macbeth himself to be followed very closely. He appeared in the background witnessing the murder of **Lady Macduff** and her children, as if he had become so isolated that he only believed what he saw with his own eyes. Another significant decision was to include **Fleance** in some of the early scenes so that, although he said nothing, a close relationship was established with his father. This made the scene where **Banquo** helps his son escape death all the more moving. It also emphasised the differences between Macbeth and Banquo: the one an isolated tyrant, the other a loving father.

ACTORS' PERSPECTIVES:
PLAYING MACBETH

Like tragic heroes, actors make choices! In this play one of the first and biggest choices an actor must make is to decide on **Macbeth**'s state of mind just before he meets the witches for the first time. Is he already ambitious to be king? Or is the message of the **Weird Sisters** the start of a whole new idea? From this decision many others follow: his attitude to **Banquo**, his superstition, and especially, his relationship with **Lady Macbeth**.

DAVID GARRICK

When the actor playing Macbeth is also the director, as was the case with David Garrick in 1744, the choice of how to play the role may be reinforced by changes to the text, too. Attitudes to texts have changed since the eighteenth century and it is unlikely that anyone would now add a dying speech to the end of *Macbeth*.

Garrick did, however, and it backed up his interpretation of Macbeth as a murderer and a tyrant whose conscience eventually catches up with him.

Garrick's Macbeth was undoubtedly on the way to hell, as his dying speech says, 'It is too late, hell drags me down. I sink …'

An eighteenth-century engraving of David Garrick as Macbeth.

It was intended to provide an important moral lesson for the audience: this is what happens to the wicked. Those watching Garrick die on the six-foot square green carpet provided for all death scenes at this time may have felt pity. They would also have felt terror. Hell was, for them, a reality.

An audience today is unlikely to see Macbeth's journey towards catastrophe in terms of heaven and hell. But we may be drawn to ask the other big question about tragic heroes: is the destruction of themselves and those around them a *waste* of human potential? Does Macbeth's tragedy lie in what he failed to achieve, as a brave and loyal subject of King Duncan? One of the big issues of the play is how far we can feel sympathy for Macbeth.

LAURENCE OLIVIER

One of the greatest twentieth-century actors, Laurence Olivier, tackled the role of Macbeth twice (and had also played **Malcolm** in the badly received 1926 production set in the First World War). He was particularly admired for his performance in the Stratford season of 1955. Critics of the time have given a memorable picture of him, saying that '… he radiates a kind of brooding sinister energy …' This Macbeth was a man haunted by the thought of murder right from the start. The **Weird Sisters'** prophecy merely stoked a fire of ruthless ambition which was already lit.

A portrait by Ruskin Spear of Laurence Olivier as Macbeth, 1955.

IAN McKELLEN

Twenty years later at Stratford, Ian McKellen also gave a performance which followed the inner progress of a man driven to power. At first Ian McKellen's Macbeth was firmly in control of his public self, able to play the part of a loyal subject of **King Duncan**. But the public mask soon began to crack and slip away. It was as if the gap between how he was seen by others and his murderous private world was too great for him to hold together. After murdering Duncan he stared at his own bloody hands with disbelief, appalled at what he had done.

He was superb in the banquet scene when the shock of seeing Banquo's ghost seemed to cut right through to his innermost being, and he collapsed with an epileptic fit. Gradually this Macbeth's private world began to fall apart as well, and he turned back to the Weird Sisters.

Desperate to know about the future, he was given only dolls and puppets, the pathetic charms and talismans of witchcraft, which he carried with him even into the final battle with **Macduff**. One theatre critic summed up Ian McKellen's performance as a 'study of evil bursting through a mask like a clown through a paper hoop.'

JONATHAN PRYCE

When Adrian Noble began working on the play in 1986 with a company of actors led by Jonathan Pryce and Sinead Cusack, he wanted to play down the supernatural in favour of an exploration of inner desires. The actors researched case studies of murderers and tried to understand their states of mind.

Jonathan Pryce has talked about this central challenge. In preparing the role he was aware of the political situation in which Macbeth acts. He remembered that in Scotland the crown did not automatically pass from father to son but to the thane (lord) who was best able to rule. Macbeth has been the saviour of his country in battle. He is an honoured member of the King's court. He is, in fact, a suitable successor to the throne. So it is not surprising that he is disappointed when Duncan makes Malcolm his heir. It is possible to see Macbeth as having both personal and patriotic reasons for claiming the crown: perhaps he is the best man to rule Scotland.

By keeping this line of thought during rehearsal an actor might see Macbeth as a complex figure, not simply evil or psychopathic, even though he commits evil deeds. As Jonathan Pryce said: 'Maybe one would say they were evil, but that evil was part of their political system.'

DEREK JACOBI

In a 1994 Royal Shakespeare
Company production, Derek Jacobi
took the title role. Throughout his
performance of Macbeth he was
painfully aware of his own moral
decline and guilt. He met the
witches for the first time with
surprise, even good humour. But
one choice after another took
away his capacity for
goodness, and isolated him.
In the end he welcomed
death, virtually impaling
himself on Macduff's
sword on the words
'Hold, enough!'

Macbeth (Jonathan Pryce)
faces the last battle in
Adrian Noble's 1986
production for the RSC.

ACTORS' PERSPECTIVES:

PLAYING LADY MACBETH

I f **Macbeth**'s character is a frightening prospect for an actor, **Lady Macbeth** is even more daunting. After only a few minutes on stage, the actress has the extraordinary speech in which Lady Macbeth calls on supernatural powers to strip her of all womanly qualities, replacing them with 'direst cruelty'. She is committed to her violent purpose. There will be no pity, no shrinking from whatever horrors become necessary. The speech is a terrifying spell, conjuring up evil power, and it is not surprising that some actresses have shied away from expressing such inhuman thoughts. Yet Lady Macbeth is also an irresistible challenge.

SARAH SIDDONS

The great Sarah Siddons (1755–1831) described her own unnerving experience as a young actress first approaching the part:

'I shut myself up as usual, when all the family were retired, and commenced my study of Lady Macbeth. I went on with tolerable composure [quite calmly], in the silence of the night, till I came to the assassination scene, when the horrors of the scene rose to a degree that made it impossible to get farther. I snatched up my candle, and hurried out of the room in a paroxysm [fit] of terror.'

This painting by Thomas Beach, 1806, shows Mrs Sarah Siddons as Lady Macbeth with John Philip Kemble as Macbeth.

Sarah Siddons went on to score one of her greatest triumphs in the role. She impressed audiences of the day as superbly intelligent, powerful and mesmerising. Those who saw it would never forget the sleep-walking scene, where Lady Macbeth acts out the murder once again and mimes pouring water desperately over her hands. One onlooker wrote: 'Well, sir, I smelt blood! I swear I smelt blood.'

Late twentieth-century audiences are probably harder to convince than those who flocked to see Mrs Siddons. We are used to a realistic style of acting on film and television and any hint of melodrama would be the death of a modern actress's portrayal of Lady Macbeth.

JUDI DENCH

Judi Dench, who played the role at Stratford in 1976 with Ian McKellen as Macbeth, found the character's motivation in ambition for her husband as well as herself. It was a twisted form of her love for him. She was attracted by the black magic he became involved in and she dabbled in satanic practices. But she was also afraid, fainting to the ground at the end of the banquet scene where Macbeth has seen **Banquo**'s ghost.

Her husband picked her up and pushed her face into a 'normal' expression as if she were a puppet or a ventriloquist's dummy, ready for the next public performance.

This understanding of Lady Macbeth, linking her intimately with her husband, was one which Judi Dench made convincingly strong. She appeared capable of everything vicious but at the same time she was vulnerable. Once Macbeth retreated into his own world of terror and tyranny she was totally lost; there was no purpose to her carrying on and her death 'at her own hand' was no surprise.

Judi Dench as Lady Macbeth with Ian McKellen as Macbeth.
Royal Shakespeare Company, 1976.

THE MACBETHS' RELATIONSHIP

How the director sees the relationship between the Macbeths affects his choice of cast. Many directors have wanted to indicate a strong sexual love between the two, which Lady Macbeth is able to use when she goads her husband into killing **King Duncan**.

Helen Mirren played a young and sexy Lady Macbeth in the 1974 RSC production, with Nicol Williamson as a satanic Macbeth. This Lady Macbeth used her sexuality to goad the ambitious Macbeth on to murder.

A highly stylised Japanese language version of the play, directed by Yukio Ninagawa, visited the National Theatre in London in 1987. The production seemed to tilt the play away from the harsh masculine world in which it so often takes place towards a much more feminine one. This was accentuated by the constant fall of cherry blossom. And Komaki Kurihara's beauty and fragility as Lady Macbeth covered up an ambition which at first appalled Macbeth and then turned him into a willing puppet of her manipulation. She showed the close links there can be between sexual attractiveness and a desire for power.

SINEAD CUSACK

Sinead Cusack played Lady Macbeth in Adrian Noble's 1986 production for the RSC. The director encouraged her, and Jonathan Pryce as her husband, to explore something of the ordinariness of evil, or at least how great evil can grow from comparatively small and simple choices and attitudes.

They looked at their relationship: Mr and Mrs Macbeth rather than the Thane of Glamis and his Lady. They began before the play starts, imagining how the Macbeths would already have been plotting, talking about the succession to the throne, convincing each other that Macbeth was the best man for the job. Sinead Cusack did not portray a 'wicked witch' but a woman obsessed by her husband. She was in no doubt that at some time they had lost their child and, in their pain, had turned in towards each other.

For Sinead Cusack, Lady Macbeth was totally ambitious for her husband, but didn't really think through where this ambition would lead them. Again and again she made wrong choices. She thought that asking to have all feelings of pity removed from her and to exercise 'direst cruelty' would be enough. She thought that she would be able to share in the killing of Duncan. But, in the end, she could not live with it. Her feelings came back to haunt her.

Sinead Cusack and Jonathan Pryce in particular showed how the Macbeths began as a couple, but by the end were facing their own individual hells. For Sinead Cusack this was seen most crucially in the killing of Duncan. Lady Macbeth, she came to feel, was completely possessed by the excitement of listening to her husband plunging the daggers into the sleeping king: they entered hell together. But from this moment they started to go their separate ways. Lady Macbeth had unlocked something in her husband that she had not bargained for: the one killing gave Macbeth the urge to do many more; for his wife it led to horror, disintegration, and finally suicide.

Sinead Cusack as Lady Macbeth in the Royal Shakespeare Company's 1986 production.

THE WEIRD SISTERS

AND THE PORTER

One of the most exciting things about exploring Shakespeare's plays is the way he makes important ideas reappear in so many unlikely forms. *Macbeth* is a play of extremes and opposites. This can be seen in the images: night and day, darkness and light, and so on. It is there in the contrasts between good kings and wicked tyrants. It can also be seen in the mutually destructive relationship of **Macbeth** and **Lady Macbeth**. And it is there in the list of characters itself: the **Weird Sisters** and the **Porter**.

At first sight there seems little connection between three witches, giving mysterious prophecies and conjuring up supernatural powers, and a drunken gatekeeper with his leering humour and the original 'Knock, knock …' jokes. But in *Macbeth* opposites tend to meet: the witches are representatives of evil, companions of the devil, and the Porter is nothing less than the keeper of the gates of hell. All represent the forces of darkness which conquer the Macbeths.

Everyone knows there are witches in *Macbeth*. Many people could quote their chanting in the opening scenes: 'When shall we three meet again …', and again in Act 4, 'Double, double, toil and trouble …' What seems familiar to us was very frightening to Shakespeare's audiences. What is the purpose of the witches?

In many early productions they were part of a spectacle: in the seventeenth and eighteenth centuries they sang and danced and even 'flew' – on wires hanging above the stage. In a world that still believed in the power of witchcraft, perhaps that was necessary as a way of making their dangers less disturbing.

The Weird Sisters – a painting by Johann Heinrich (Henry) Fuseli.

In many twentieth-century productions they have become more human: old women searching the battlefields for treasures perhaps. But the challenge of *Macbeth* is to make the Weird Sisters both human and strange, believable yet terrifying at the same time.

Trevor Nunn's production in 1976 placed the witches in a world where they would be believed and feared. The third witch, a young woman speaking like a spiritualist's medium, seeing visions that terrified her, took us into her own frantic imagination. Later, when Macbeth asked for more visions, more proof of his safety, they used the bits and pieces of childhood – dolls and puppets – to summon up the spirits.

This connection of the witches with children was taken up much more fully in Adrian Noble's 1986 production. Here the third witch had a child of her own – in contrast to Macbeth, whose child was dead. Later, the ghostly apparitions Macbeth asks for were again children, who then became **Macduff**'s children, murdered at Macbeth's command. It was as if Macbeth was haunted by his childlessness. Not having children puts the Macbeths in their own despairing hell.

In Trevor Nunn's 1976 RSC production, Ian McDiarmid made the Porter a foul-mouthed Glaswegian, a demonic stand-up comic, cracking jokes and putting off opening the gate to the fury of Macduff waiting outside. But these are no ordinary jokes: they are about lying and deceit, truth and falsehood – major themes of the play. The Macbeths have welcomed **Duncan** under their roof as loyal subjects and honest hosts. Now they have killed him and with that murderous deception they have entered the hell whose gates the Porter will now open. It is a hell they will never leave.

'Knock, knock, knock. Who's there? an equivocator.' Ian McDiarmid as the Porter. Royal Shakespeare Company, 1976

INDEX